100 EASY PIANO TUNES

Philip Hawthorn and Anya Suschitzky

Edited by Anthony Marks and Jenny Tyler

Designed and illustrated by Simone Abel and Kim Blundell

Arrangements by Sharon Armstrong and Anya Suschitzky

Original music by Sharon Armstrong, Anthony Marks and Anya Suschitzky

Music engraving by Poco Ltd, Letchworth, Herts

About this book

This is a book of tunes which you can play on your piano or electronic keyboard. It will help you to improve your skill as a player, and also read and understand music better.

In this book there are folk songs, tunes from classical music and jazz tunes. Some you won't have heard before because they have been specially written. There are also tunes for two players.

The tunes get harder as you go through the book. The first tunes are ones you can play without moving the position of your hands. The tunes at the end are more difficult.

Some pieces of music contain symbols or words that you may not have seen before. Every time a new music symbol or word appears, it will be explained in a box at the foot of the page.

During the last 250 years there have been lots of amazing and curious pianos made, such as one that plays itself. You can find out about these on some of the pages in this book.

You can find out about composers, such as Beethoven, and their music. There are lots of interesting facts about the tunes in the book. There is also a section about piano records which you can listen to.

Sur le pont d'Avignon

This is a very old French tune. The title means "On the Bridge of Avignon".

French

Note names

On the right is a picture to remind you of the names of the white notes on your keyboard, and where the notes are written on the music.

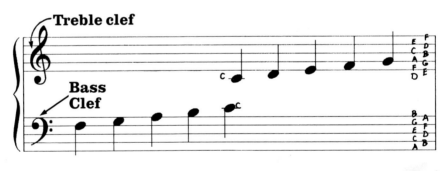

Treble clef

Bass Clef

Right hand notes on this staff.

Left hand notes on this one.

This note is the C nearest to the middle of your keyboard. It is called middle C.

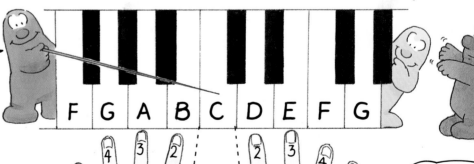

F G A B C D E F G

Finger numbers

Each tune in this book has numbers in it to tell you which fingers to use to play notes. This picture shows you which number stands for which finger.

For the first few tunes in the book, you start with your thumbs on middle C.

4

Yankee Doodle

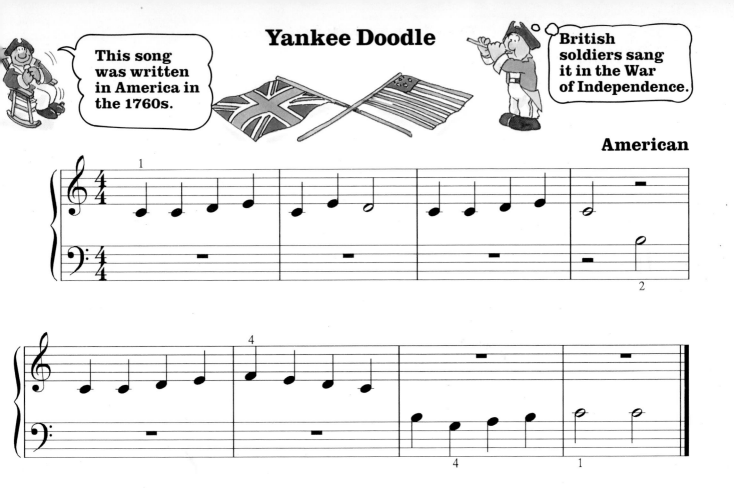

Note lengths

Below you can see three types of note. Each one lasts for a different number of beats.

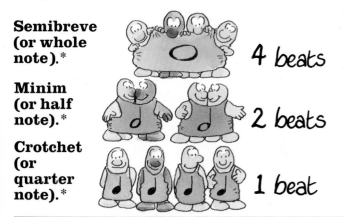

Semibreve (or whole note).* — 4 beats

Minim (or half note).* — 2 beats

Crotchet (or quarter note).* — 1 beat

Rests

When you see a rest on either staff, it tells you not to play with that hand for a certain number of beats. Below are three types of rest, with their lengths.

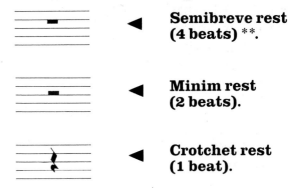

◄ **Semibreve rest (4 beats) **.**

◄ **Minim rest (2 beats).**

◄ **Crotchet rest (1 beat).**

Time signatures

The numbers at the start of each tune are called the time signature. This tells you how many beats there are in each bar, and the length of the beats.

This number tells you that there are four beats in every bar.

This number tells you that the beats are crotchet length.

* The names in brackets are what the notes are called in North America.
** This symbol is also used to show a whole bar rest of any number of beats.

5

Bobby Shaftoe

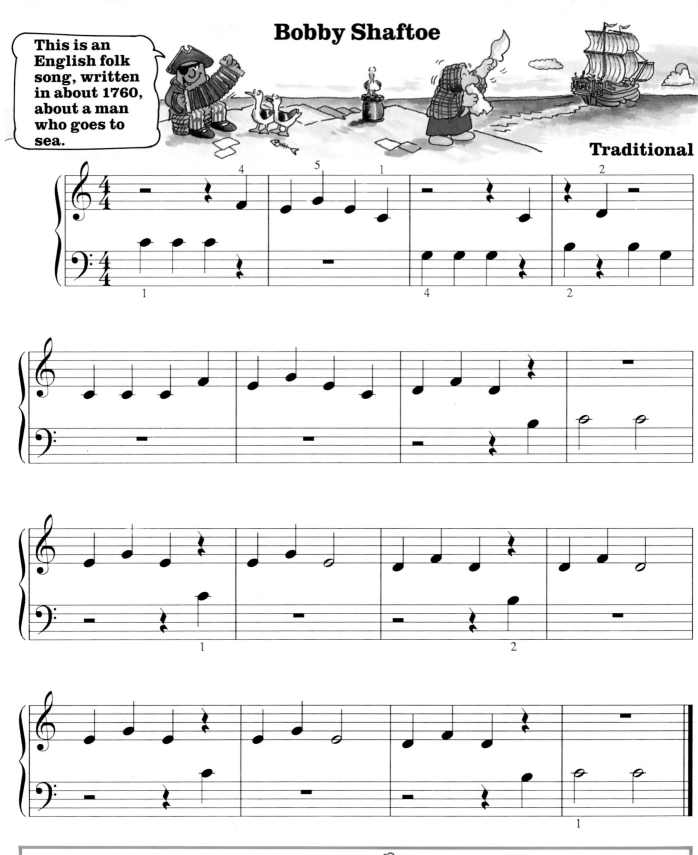

Traditional

Row, row, row the boat

This tune has dotted minims in it. You can find out about them below.

Scottish

Dotted minims

A dot after a note increases its length by half as much again. A minim lasts for two beats, so a dot adds one beat to its length.

A minim is two beats long.

Half a minim is one beat.

A dotted minim is three beats.

This tune has two silent bars. For these, count three beats in your head.

7

On eagles' wings

Quavers

A quaver is half a beat long. Clap the rhythm on the right as you say the words. The quavers are the same length as each other, don't rush them.

Quick qua - ver claps

Quavers can be written on their own, like this.

The dinosaur and the dormouse

Amazing pianos

In the 1860s there were pianos which played themselves called pianolas, or player-pianos. There are some still around today.

9

In this tune, you play one of the black notes on your piano. Find out more below.

Oh, dear, what can the matter be?

This tune was written in Scotland around the year 1770.

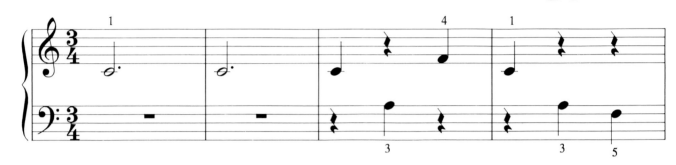

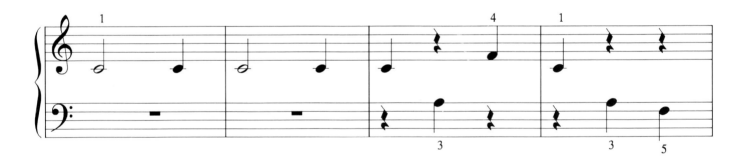

A black note

The black note in this tune is the one below B. It is called B flat. In the music, it has a ♭ sign in front of it.

Before you play, put the second finger of your left hand on the B♭ note instead of the B note.

12

The bell ringers

This tune has another black note in it. You can find out about it at the bottom of the page.

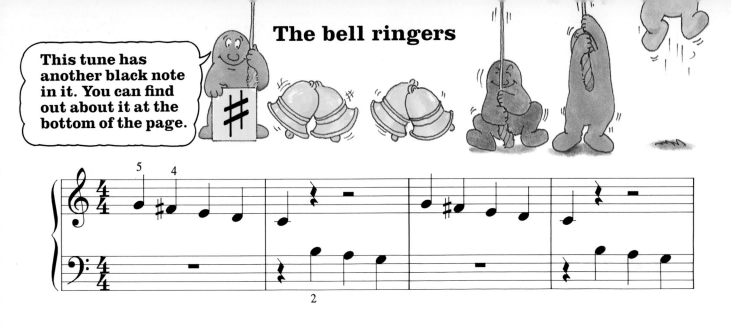

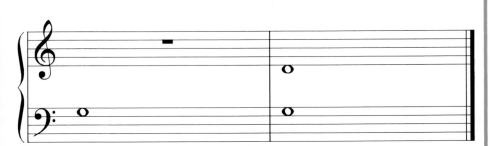

Another black note

The black note in this tune is called F sharp. It is the one above the F note and has a sharp sign, ♯, in front of it.

Put the fourth finger of your right hand on the F♯ note before you play.

Accidentals

A sharp or flat before a note is called an accidental. You play the note sharp or flat each time it appears in that bar. The barline cancels the accidental.

This sign is a natural. It also cancels sharps and flats.

13

Apache rain dance

Strings of notes

Sometimes you have to play lots of notes running up or down the keyboard. Here are two exercises for your right hand to help you to know which fingers to use.

Going up...

Start with your thumb on C and play the white notes using the 3-4-3 finger pattern above.

Thumb under finger.

14

Ho-la-hi

German

Playing loudly

The words for loudness are based on the Italian word *forte* (for-tay) which means loud or strong. Press the keys firmly when you play *forte*.

16

Away in a manger

This tune has letters to tell you to play it softly.

There are more carols to play on pages 26-27.

W. J. Kirkpatrick

Playing softly

The words telling you to play softly are based on the Italian word for "softly", *piano*. Press the keys gently to play *piano*.

mezzo piano means quite soft.

piano means soft.

pianissimo means very soft.

17

Haunted house

The notes in this tune have two sorts of dots. Find out what they mean below.

Dotted crotchets

A dotted crotchet is one and a half beats long. Here you can see how to play the right rhythm.

Clap on the beats that are underlined.

Playing staccato

When a note has a dot over or under it, play it short. Take your finger off quickly once you have played the note. This is called playing staccato.

18

At the fair

This tune is played very smoothly. Find out more below.

Playing legato

When notes on different lines or spaces are linked by a curved line, it means you play them very smoothly. This is called playing legato.

To play legato, press each note just before you take your finger off the previous one.

The notes linked by curved lines in this way are called phrases.

19

Where, oh where has my little dog gone?

English

This song, first sung in the late 1800s, was also known as "The Dutchman's Wee Dog."

Amazing pianos

These two pianos were shown at the 1851 Great Exhibition in London.

This "twin semi-cottage piano" was invented by John Champion Jones.

William Jenkin invented a piano for taking on ships. It collapsed to only 34cm deep.

20

Down in the valley

You have to play some of this tune twice. Find out more below.

There is an Italian word at the start of this tune telling you how fast to play.

Allegro

Traditional

How fast to play

Words written at the beginning of a tune tell you at what speed (tempo) you have to play it. Sometimes the words are Italian. This is because music was first printed in Italy. Below are some words to tell you different tempos.

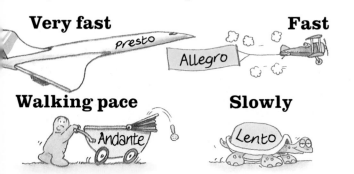

Very fast — Presto

Fast — Allegro

Walking pace — Andante

Slowly — Lento

Repeating music from the beginning

The sign below is called a repeat mark. It means you go back to the beginning and play the tune again.

You only play the last bar of this tune once.

You ignore the repeat mark the second time.

The grand old duke of York

There are sharp signs at the start of this tune (see below).

English

Key signatures

The ♯ written next to the clefs is called a key signature. You play F♯ instead of F all the way through the tune.

This tune is in the key of G major.

The key signature saves you writing a ♯ sign each time there is an F.

Remember, extra naturals, flats or sharps only apply to the bar in which they appear.

22

Anna's gerbils

You can find out what allegro means on page 21.

There are two accidentals in this tune.

Allegro

24

German national anthem

Haydn

26

We wish you a merry Christmas

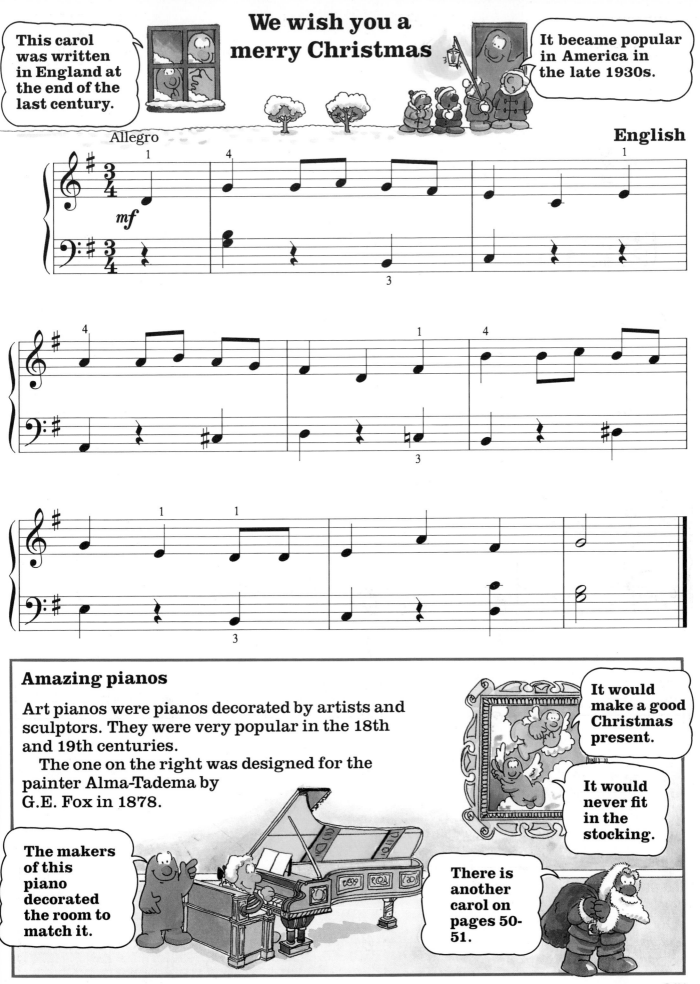

This carol was written in England at the end of the last century.

It became popular in America in the late 1930s.

Allegro

English

mf

Amazing pianos

Art pianos were pianos decorated by artists and sculptors. They were very popular in the 18th and 19th centuries.

The one on the right was designed for the painter Alma-Tadema by G.E. Fox in 1878.

It would make a good Christmas present.

It would never fit in the stocking.

The makers of this piano decorated the room to match it.

There is another carol on pages 50-51.

Space walk rag

Rags were popular at the beginning of the century.

The sign ⅞ is a quaver rest. Pause half a beat.

Playing rag rhythms

Rags have a special rhythm, known as ragtime. Here are some hints to help you play ragtime well.

Try not to rush. Make the music sound relaxed and keep a steady beat.

Make the second and fourth beats of the bar slightly longer.

This jerky rhythm is called syncopation.

29

Au clair de la lune

This tune was written by a French composer called Lully in about 1680.

The title is French. It means "by the light of the moon".

French

Amazing pianos

Johann Pape (1789 – 1875) had a piano factory in Paris. He built many unusual pianos. On the right are two which were strange shapes.

Frère Jacques

French

How to play a round

You can play this tune on your own, or you can play it as a "round" with a friend.

One of you starts playing from the beginning. When you get to the letter B, the second player starts from the beginning whilst the first continues to the end.

Two people playing on one keyboard

If two people play on one keyboard, this picture shows you which notes each of them could play.

Middle C

Player 1   Player 2

Using a tape recorder

Instead of playing the round with two people, you could use a tape recorder and play both parts yourself.

Walking

Antonio Diabelli

More about phrases

Some music is written in phrases, like words are spoken in sentences. Lift your hand slightly after a phrase, before playing the next one. It is a bit like taking a breath.

32

Clementine

Dotted quavers

A dot after a quaver increases it by half as much again. Half a quaver is called a semiquaver. A dotted quaver lasts for three semiquavers.

34

"From the New World"

Some parts of this tune get louder, and some get softer. Find out more below.

Dvořák was a Czech composer. He lived from 1841 to 1904.

Dvořák

Getting louder

This symbol between the staves means you get gradually louder as you play. It is called *crescendo* (cre-shen-do). Sometimes written *cresc.*

You start to get louder here.

You stop getting louder here.

The tune continues on the next page.

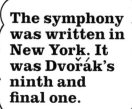

The symphony was written in New York. It was Dvořák's ninth and final one.

At that time, many Europeans thought of America as a "new world".

Parts of the music are based on American Indian folk music, spirituals and rags.

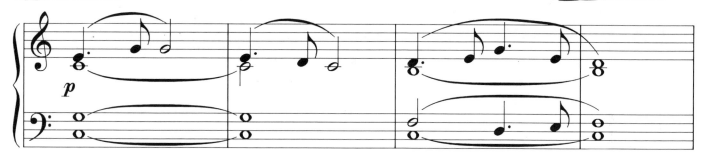

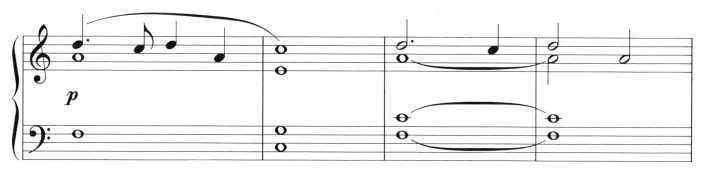

Getting softer

This symbol tells you to play gradually more softly. It is called *diminuendo* (dim-in-u-en-do). It is sometimes written as *dim*.

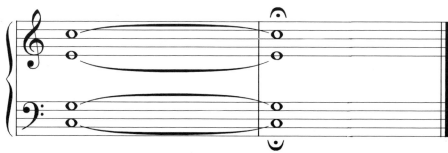

Remembering the symbols

To remember what each symbol means, look at the gap between the lines.

Gap getting bigger means get louder.

Gap getting smaller means get softer.

It's like turning the volume up or down.

Autumn

This tune is in 6/8 time. There are six quavers to each bar, in two groups of three.

Cantabile means "in a flowing style". It is Italian for "singing".

38

Winter

There are tunes for the other two seasons on the next page.

Ledger lines

Ledger lines can be written above or below either staff. These are the ledger line notes in this piece:

Below the bass clef:

B A G F

Below the treble clef:

E D

The notes below the treble clef could be written in the bass clef. But they are written this way to tell you to play them with your right hand.

39

Spring

Part of this tune is an echo. Play it mezzo forte, then piano.

Amazing pianos

This piano was called a "perpendicular piano". It was invented in 1878 by William Percival.

There is one keyboard for each hand.

This was so that the player could face the audience and sing.

Summer

There are new ledger line notes in this tune. Find out more below.

Andante

More ledger line notes

In this piece there are two ledger line notes above the right hand staff and two above the left hand staff.

B   A

D   E

Remember, key signatures and accidentals also apply to notes on ledger lines.

41

Wedding march

This tune was written by a German composer called Mendelssohn. It is often played at weddings.

You have to repeat part of this tune. Find out more below.

Mendelssohn

Fine

D.C. al Fine

A new kind of repeat

Fine ("fee-nay") is Italian for "the end". *D.C.* stands for *Da Capo. Da Capo al Fine* means play from the top until you reach the *Fine* sign.

Start at the beginning and play through the piece once until you reach *D.C. al Fine*.

Then start again and play through to the *Fine* sign.

The thick barline shows you where to stop.

42

Daisy Bell

Harry Dacre

This tune is about a couple being married and going away on a tandem.

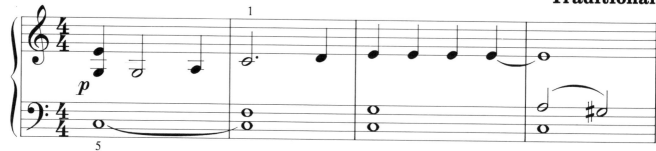

This tune is from a song called a "spiritual".

You can find out more about spirituals below.

Traditional

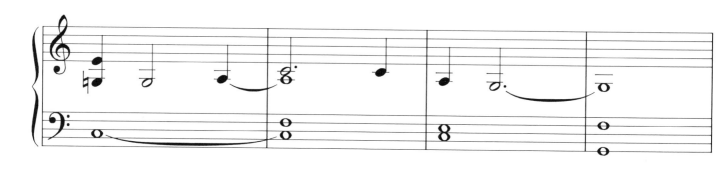

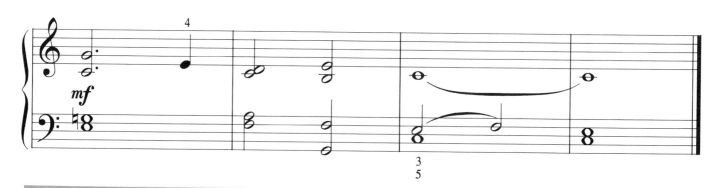

Spirituals

Spirituals were first sung in America in the middle of the last century. They were usually sung by black slaves.

Lots of other styles of music are based on spirituals.

These include jazz, ragtime, blues, soul and gospel music.

Kum by yah

Traditional

Amazing pianos

In 1866 a piano was invented by a man called Millward. As well as the keyboard, it also contained a sofa, a desk, a mirror, lots of drawers, a wash basin, a sewing box, a writing table and cupboards for soap, towels, shaving equipment and bedclothes.

45

Riding on a donkey

Allegretto means "play not quite as fast as allegro".

This tune has notes with accents. Find out more below.

Traditional

Accents

An accent tells you to play the note by pressing harder and more quickly than usual.

How quickly you press a note is called the attack.

Accent notes are louder than normal.

Remember, this note is a semiquaver.

The rhythm on the left is twice as fast as the one on the right.

46

Toreador's song

This tune is from an opera called "Carmen", set in Spain. A toreador is a bullfighter.

Bizet was a French composer. He lived from 1838 to 1875.

Allegro

Bizet

Opera

An opera is like a play except that nearly all the words are sung.

There is an orchestra in front of the stage to play the music.

Operas were first written about the year 1600. Some composers who have written opera are Gluck, Wagner, Verdi and Mozart.

From the "Surprise" Symphony

Lullaby

This tune was written by the German composer Johannes Brahms. He lived from 1833 to 1897.

This tune has some small notes like these. Find out more below.

Lento

Brahms

Small notes

These small notes are called grace notes. You play them as quickly as you can.

Grace notes are often written as semiquavers. They are played quickly before the main note.

You play these just before the second beat.

Grace notes help to make the music more interesting.

52

54

Scarborough fair

This tune is from an old English folk song.

56

A classic duet (part B)

On these two pages is a tune for you to play with a friend. One plays part A and the other part B at the same time.

Tunes for two players are duets.

It will help if you both count a bar together before you start.

Octaves and scales

An octave is the distance from any note to the next one with the same name. A scale is a set of eight notes played one after the other covering an octave.

This is the scale of C major.

Find out more about scales on page 62.

58

A classic duet (part A)

Be careful! This part has a treble clef for the left hand.

You can find out what this means below.

mf

Playing up an octave

Part of this music is played an octave higher than it is written. Find out more on the right.

When you see middle C..

.. you play an octave above it.

In the ninth bar, the right hand begins on the third D above middle C.

Melody in A minor
(part B)

Melody in A minor (part A)

Music help

On this page you can see all the music symbols, words and theory that are in the book. The index on page 128 will show where in the book they are explained.

Key signatures and scales

On the right you can see the key signatures used in this book. The key signature also shows you which sharps and flats are in that particular scale. For example, in the scale of G major (which begins and ends on G) there is an F#.

C major

This is the same key signature as A minor.

G major

F major

D major

Bb major

Words for speed and attack

Here are the Italian words which tell you how quickly to play, and how to press the keys.

adagio	slowly	*lento*	slowly
allegretto	fairly quickly	*moderato*	at a moderate speed
allegro	quickly	*pesante*	heavily
andante	at a walking pace	*presto*	very fast
a tempo	return to original speed	*rallentando (rall.)*	slowing down
cantabile	singing	*ritenuto (rit.)*	held back
grazioso	gracefully	*staccato*	short
legato	smoothly	*tenuto*	held
leggiero	lightly		

Words for loud and soft

The list below is to remind you about the symbols which tell you how loudly to play.

pp	very softly
p	softly
mp	fairly softly
mf	fairly loudly
f	loudly
ff	very loudly
crescendo	getting louder
diminuendo	getting softer

You can find out about these on pages 16 and 17.

...and these on pages 36 and 37.

Ledger lines

These staves show you what note names different ledger lines have.

Listening to piano music

Here you can find out about classical and jazz piano music and some famous pianists.

Classical piano pieces

Below are some interesting piano pieces you can find on record, cassette or compact disc.

Bach	Preludes and Fugues
Beethoven	Concerto no. 5 in E flat
	Piano sonatas: "Moonlight", "Appassionata", "Pathétique"
Brahms	Piano Concerto no. 2
Chopin	Waltzes, Etudes, Nocturnes and Polonaises
Debussy	Children's Corner Suite
Gershwin	Piano Concerto in F
Grieg	Piano Concerto in A minor
Joplin	Rags (including "The Entertainer", "Maple Leaf Rag")
Liszt	"Consolation" in D♭
Mozart	Piano Concertos nos. 21, 22 and 23
	Sonata in A major
Rachmaninov	Prelude in C♯ minor
Satie	"Trois Gymnopedies"
Schubert	Piano Quintet in A major ("The Trout")
Schumann	Scenes from Childhood
Tchaikovsky	Piano Concerto no. 1

Classical pianists

Below are the names of some of the best known modern pianists. They have recorded a lot of music, including many of the pieces on the left.

Peter Donohoe
Artur Rubinstein
Vladimir Horowitz
Clifford Curzon
Vladimir Ashkenazy
Daniel Barenboim
Moura Lympany

Jazz pianists

Below are the names of some jazz pianists. They have made many recordings. Most of them have had their own bands. They each play music in their own style.

Jelly Roll Morton
Oscar Peterson
'Fats' Waller
Duke Ellington
Dave Brubeck
Chick Corea
Keith Jarrett

Amazing piano music

A musician named Czerny arranged a piece of music for eight pianos and 16 players.

The longest piano piece is called "The Well Tuned Piano" by La Monte Young. It is nearly four and a half hours long.

In another piece by La Monte Young, there was a music instruction to feed the piano on hay and water before playing it.

Music quiz

Here is a quiz based on facts in this book. There is only one correct answer to each question. You can find the information you need to answer Section 1 on pages 4-63 and the information you need to answer Section 2 on pages 68-125. The answers are at the bottom of page 66.

Section 1

1. What is an octave?
a) a group of eight semiquavers (sixteenth notes)
b) the distance between two notes of the same name
c) a shape with eight sides

2. Yankee Doodle was sung by:
a) soldiers during the American War of Independence
b) miners during the American gold rush of 1849
c) blues singers at the beginning of the 20th century

3. How many quavers (eighth notes) are there in a dotted minim (dotted half note) ?
a) three
b) six
c) four

4. Who wrote the *"Surprise" Symphony*?
a) Haydn
b) Brahms
c) Pachelbel

5. What does this sign > mean?
a) staccato
b) accent
c) legato

6. What is this sign ♮ ?
a) a sharp
b) a flat
c) a natural

7. What are ledger lines?
a) the lines that join two or more quavers (eighth notes) together
b) lines for notes above or below the staff
c) the five lines of the staff on which the notes are written

8. The biggest piano ever made weighed:
a) 1.25 tonnes (1.23 tons)
b) 3 tonnes (2.95) tons
c) 1000kg (2200lbs)

9. Who wrote the *"New World" Symphony*?
a) Beethoven
b) Bizet
c) Dvořák

10. A pianola is:
a) a kind of Italian food
b) a piano that plays itself
c) the left pedal on a piano

11. Syncopation is:
a) an accent on the "off beat"
b) a kind of rag
c) a dotted rhythm that continues throughout a piece

12. When were the first operas written?
a) around 1500
b) around 1600
c) around 1700

13. Which of these composers was born first?
a) Mendelssohn
b) Haydn
c) Lully

14. What is a duet?
a) a dance
b) a tune for two players
c) part of a piece of music that is played twice

15. What does *legato* mean?
a) smoothly
b) slowly
c) softly

Section 2

16. Who wrote the opera *Don Giovanni*?
a) Schubert
b) Mozart
c) Bach

17. What does *cantabile* mean?
a) quickly
b) singing
c) softly

18. Who was Clara Wieck's husband?
a) Schumann
b) Handel
c) Brahms

19. The notes on a harpsichord are produced by:
a) hitting the strings
b) plucking the strings
c) bowing the strings

20. Which piece of music is also known as *The Blacksmith*?
a) Don Giovanni
b) Greensleeves
c) Pipe and drum

21. What is a musette
a) an instrument like the bagpipes
b) an ancient god of music
c) a kind of decoration or ornament

22. Oratorio is:
a) someone who speaks in public
b) an Italian word which tells you to play loudly and confidently
c) a large piece for choir and orchestra

23. Who wrote the *Trout Quintet*?
a) Leopold Mozart
b) Schubert
c) Tchaikovsky

24. How many sharps are in the scale of G major?
a) one
b) two
c) three

25. Who wrote the *Goldberg Variations*?
a) Bach
b) Goldberg
c) Mozart

26. Accidentals are:
a) mistakes made by the performer
b) mistakes made by the composer
c) extra sharps, flats or naturals added to the staff

Quiz continued

27. A sharp
a) raises a note by a semitone
b) lowers a note by a semitone
c) raises a note by a tone

28. What does *mezzo forte* mean?
a) less loudly
b) fairly loudly
c) fairly quietly

29. What are dynamics?
a) another word for the piano's pedals
b) signs for fast and slow playing
c) signs for loud and soft playing

30. Which of the following composers wrote several famous ballets?
a) Haydn
b) Beethoven
c) Tchaikovsky

31. The harpsichord is:
a) an early harp
b) a kind of chord
c) a keyboard instrument

32. A suite is:
a) a group of dances
b) a kind of French dessert
c) a kind of dance

33. Where was was Beethoven born?
a) France
b) USA
c) Germany

34. Who wrote the oratorio *Judas Maccabeus*?
a) Brahms
b) Handel
c) Judas Maccabeus

35. Who wrote *Moments musicaux*?
a) Beethoven
b) Schubert
c) Haydn

36. Which of these dances is not in $\frac{3}{4}$ time?
a) minuet
b) waltz
c) march

37. Who wrote *Album for the Young*?
a) Leopold Mozart
b) La Monte Young
c) Schumann

38. What are *Lieder*?
a) short pieces for solo piano
b) dynamics
c) songs for voice and piano

39. What is an alberti bass?
a) An extra octave of low notes on a keyboard instrument
b) a low piano stool
c) a special pattern of notes

40. Who wrote *Papillons*?
a) Chopin
b) Beethoven
c) Schumann

Answers:

38.c) 39.c) 40.c)

31.c) 32.a) 33.c) 34.b) 35.b) 36.c) 37.c)

24.a) 25.a) 26.c) 27.a) 28.b) 29.c) 30.c)

17.b) 18.a) 19.b) 20.b) 21.a) 22.c) 23.b)

10.b) 11.a) 12.b) 13.c) 14.b) 15.a) 16.b)

1.b) 2.a) 3.b) 4.a) 5.b) 6.c) 7.b) 8.a) 9.c)

This section has lots more tunes for you to play on the piano or electronic keyboard, including some more duets near the end of the book. Some of the tunes are more difficult than those on pages 4-61 and may need more practice.

There are some scales and arpeggios on pages 114-115 which will help you to improve your playing. If you come across any new Italian words or music directions in this section you can look them up in "Music help" on page 62.

This section contains plenty of new hints on piano technique and suggestions of music to listen to. You will also find more information on different kinds of keyboard instruments and composers who have written for them.

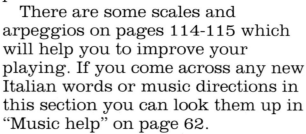

Carefree

This tune contains an accidental called C sharp. You can find out more about accidentals below.

Sharps and flats

The sharps and flats at the beginning of a tune are called the key signature. They tell you which notes to play sharp or flat throughout the tune.

A sharp raises a note by a half step or semitone (see page 114).

A flat lowers a note by a half step or semitone.

Accidentals

Sharps, flats and naturals that are not in the key signature are called accidentals. They are added to the staff in front of the note they change.

An accidental only applies to the notes in the bar in which it appears. In the next bar you go back to the original key signature.

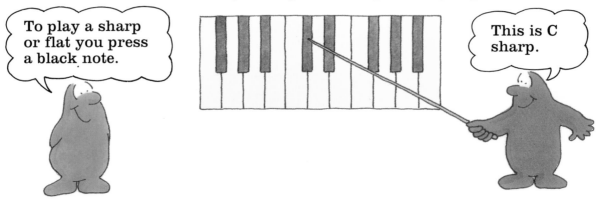

To play a sharp or flat you press a black note.

This is C sharp.

When the saints

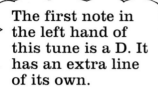

The first note in the left hand of this tune is a D. It has an extra line of its own.

When a note is higher or lower than the staff, it uses extra lines, called ledger lines. Find out more below.

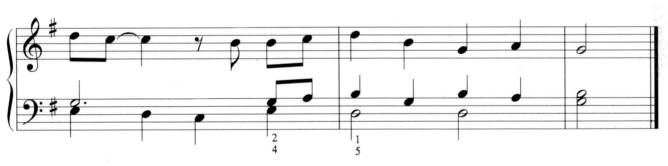

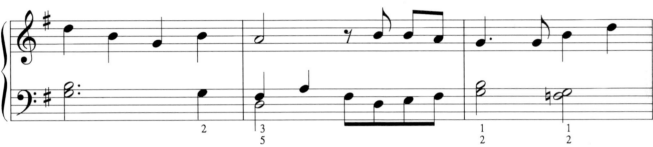

Ledger lines

To find out which note to play, count up or down from the last note on the staff like this.

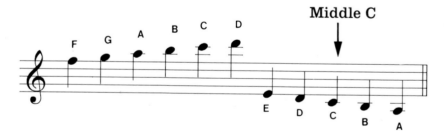

Middle C

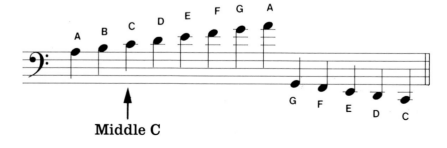

Middle C

Lullaby

Lucy Locket

Sliding song

This tune has a few rests in it. You can find out more about rests below.

Rests

This rest lasts as long as a quaver or eighth note*.

This one lasts as long as a crotchet or quarter note*.

This one lasts as long as a minim or half note*.

*These are the names used in North America.

German folk song

This tune has instructions called dynamics. Dynamics tell you how loud or soft to play.

mp is short for *mezzo piano* which means "fairly quietly". You can find out more about dynamics below and on the next page.

Dynamics

Crescendo (cresc.) means "get louder". Sometimes the sign below is used instead of the word.

Diminuendo (dim.) means "get softer". Sometimes the sign below is used instead of the word.

The train is a comin' in

This tune is a spiritual, a kind of American folk song.

You can find out what the time signature of this tune means below.

Time signatures

$\frac{2}{2}$ means there are two minims in each bar. It is sometimes written like this.

$\frac{4}{4}$ means there are four crotchet beats in each bar. It is sometimes written like this.

This time signature tells you there are six quaver beats in each bar.

More about dynamics

Piano (p) tells you to play quietly.

Mezzo forte (mf) tells you to play fairly loudly.

Forte (f) tells you to play loudly.

Singing tune

Adagio means "slowly" (see page 62 for a list of all the Italian words in the book). You can find out about repeat signs below.

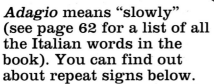

This sign is a slur. You play the notes joined by a slur as smoothly as possible (see page 85).

Repeats

These are repeat signs.

When you come to a repeat you go back to the beginning (or the last repeat sign) and play the music once again.

74

Theme from the Trout Quintet

This tune is by the Austrian composer Schubert (1797-1828). *Andante* means "at a walking pace".

The *Trout Quintet* was written for a violin, a viola, a cello, a double bass and a piano.

Minuet

Two by two

A curved line that joins two notes of the same pitch* is called a tie. To play tied notes press the key for the first note, and hold it until the end of the second note.

A dot after a note or rest means it lasts for half its length again.

* The pitch of a note is how high or low it is.

Warming up

Playing this tune will help your fingers warm up so that they work better when you play tunes.

Try to play this tune as smoothly as possible. Playing smoothly is called *legato* (see page 85).

Getting strong

This tune will help you to strengthen your fingers.

Play it slowly at first, and increase your speed gradually.

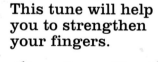

March

English minuet

Cradle song

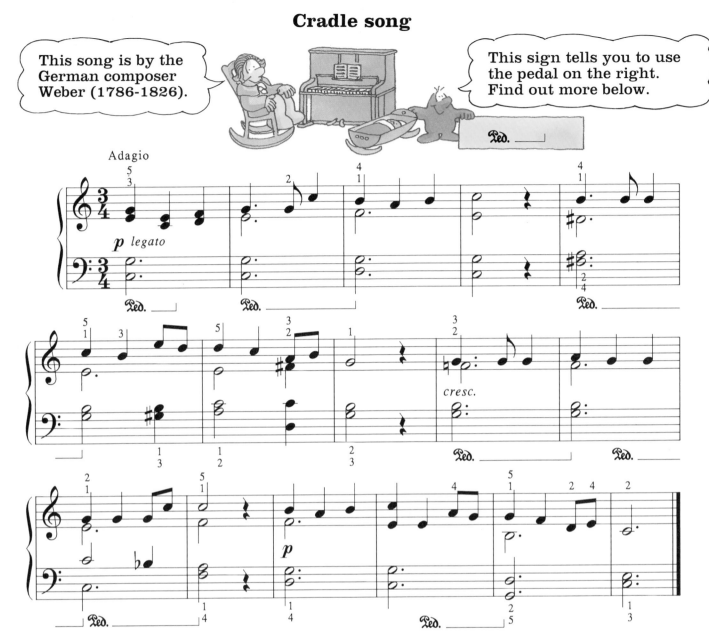

Using the sustaining pedal*

On the piano, the pedal on the right is called the sustaining pedal. It helps you move smoothly between two notes or chords. When you press it, the notes you have played will continue to sound. This is called sustaining. You can then move to the next note without making a break in the music.

*You can find out more about the sustaining pedal on page 109.

Minuet

This tune is by the French composer Rameau (1683-1764).

It was written for the harpsichord. You can find out more about the harpsichord on page 93.

Minuet

This tune was written by Leopold Mozart. He was the father of Wolfgang Amadeus Mozart, who wrote the tunes on pages 77, 98 and 116.

This is a triplet. It tells you to fit three notes into one beat.

Hymn tune

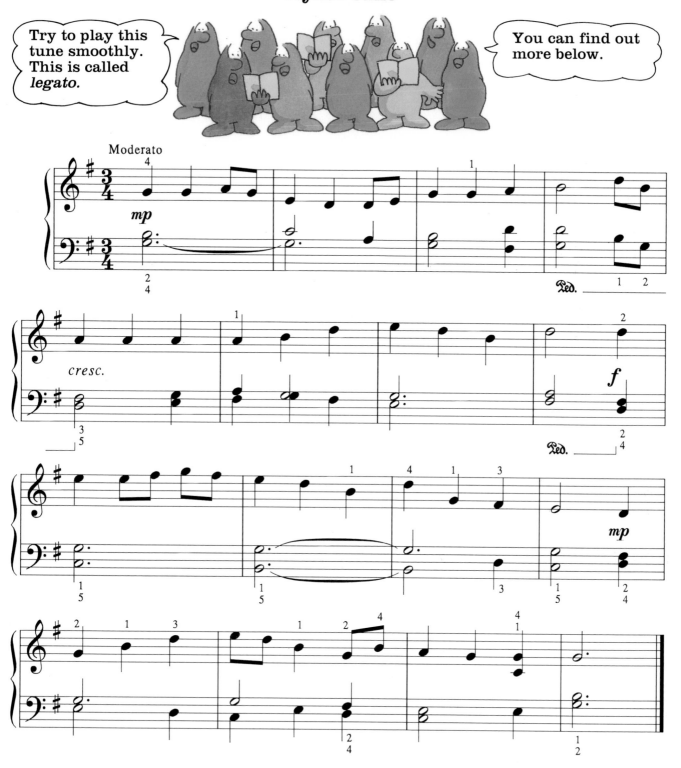

Playing legato

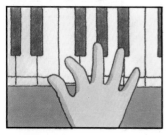

To play legato, you keep your finger down on one key until you press the key for the next note.

It helps if you keep your fingers close to the keyboard when you are playing legato.

The happy hare

This sign is a pause. You hold the note with the pause above it for about half its length again.

There is a special kind of repeat in this tune. Find out more below.

First-time bars and second-time bars

The first time through, you play the first-time bar.

When you repeat, leave out the first-time bar and play the second-time bar instead.

Then continue with the rest of the tune.

Burlesque

Try, try, try again

This is a *staccato* note. Play notes like this as short as possible.

This is an accented note. Notes with accents sound louder and more important than other notes. You can find out more below.

Accents and staccatos

To play notes with accents and staccatos, you press the keys a bit harder and more quickly than usual.

If you are playing a staccato note, you should also lift your finger as soon as possible, and make a break before the next note.

88

Lilliburlero

This is a famous Irish folk tune.

Fanfare

A fanfare is a short piece which is often played on trumpets. Fanfares are used for processions and celebrations of important people.

Maestoso means "grandly".

Liza Jane

This tune is an American folk song.

Moderato

mf

Listening to piano music

Most famous composers have written music for the piano or earlier keyboard instruments such as the harpsichord. You can find recordings of many of these pieces in the library or record shop. Mozart (1756-1791) wrote lots of sonatas and concertos for the piano. Try listening to piano concertos no.25 and no.27.

Bach (1685-1750) wrote music for the harpsichord (see page 93), the organ (see page 111), and the clavichord (an early form of the piano). Some of this music can be played on the piano. Try listening to *The Well-Tempered Clavier* and the *Goldberg Variations.* You can find out more about piano music on page 96.

A piano concerto is for a piano and orchestra. A piano sonata is for a piano alone.

Happy march

The conquering hero

This tune is by Handel (1685-1759). It is from his oratorio *Judas Maccabeus*. An oratorio is a piece for a choir and an orchestra on a religious subject.

D.C. al Fine means you go back to the beginning and play the music again. Stop when you reach the word *Fine.*

The harpsichord and the piano

The first harpsichords were built about five hundred years ago. The notes of a harpsichord are fairly quiet. Each key is linked to a piece of feather quill or plastic called a plectrum. When the keys are pressed, the plectrums pluck the strings.

When pianos were developed in the early 18th century, they became more popular than harpsichords. This is because they could play louder and longer notes than harpsichords, and because it was possible to vary the way the notes sounded.

The last rose of summer

This is an Irish folk song.

On the little hearth

This lullaby was first sung by European Jews on their way to the USA. Look out for the first- and second-time bars (see page 86).

Lullaby

Listening to piano music

During the 19th century, the piano became very popular. Composers such as Beethoven, Schubert, Schumann, Chopin and Liszt wrote lots of difficult music which was played in concerts by very good pianists called "virtuosi". Some also wrote shorter, more simple pieces for people to play at home. Schubert, who composed the tune on this page, wrote many piano sonatas and shorter pieces for piano such as *Impromptus*, *Moments musicaux*, and waltzes. He also wrote over 600 songs for voice and piano called *Lieder*, many of which have very good piano parts.

96

Smooth snakes

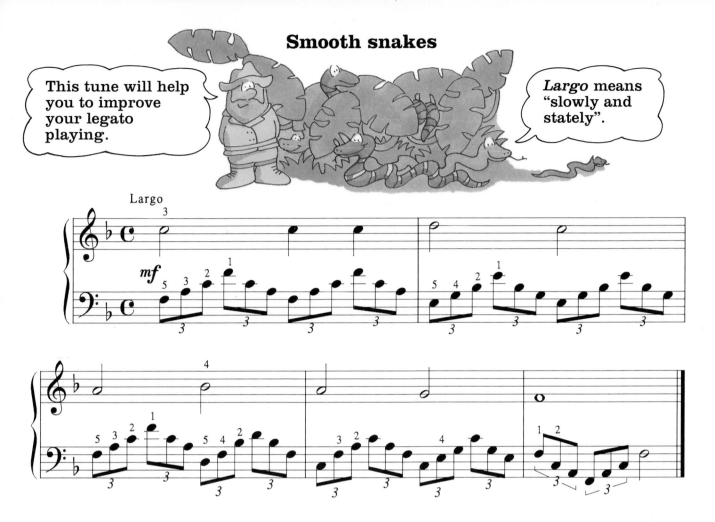

This tune will help you to improve your legato playing.

Largo means "slowly and stately".

Chords and arpeggios

The tune on this page contains arpeggios in the left hand part. Arpeggios are the notes of a chord which are spread out so that you play one at a time, either from the bottom up or from the top down. There is more about arpeggios and the scales that go with them on pages 114-115.

Sometimes chords are arranged to form a pattern called an alberti bass, in which the bottom note of the chord is played first, then the top note, then the middle note, and then the top note again. The alberti bass is named after Domenico Alberti, who often wrote bass lines like this.

Here is an arpeggio

Here is part of an alberti bass. The tune on page 96 contains an alberti bass.

You might need to play arpeggios and alberti basses separately, until you can play all the notes.

arpeggio

alberti bass

Là ci darem la mano

Fingerings

The pieces in this book tell you which fingers to use. This helps you to place your hand in a position where you will be able to play all the notes. Many of the fingerings tell you to tuck your thumb under your hand. This helps you to change the position of your hand. Playing scales and arpeggios (see pages 114-115) will also help you to tuck your thumb under your hand.

Minuet

This tune is by the German composer Bach (1685-1750), who came from a large family of musicians.

Bach wrote lots of music for the clavichord, the harpsichord and the organ. You can find out more about his music on page 91.

Theme from Beethoven's Violin Concerto

This tune is by Beethoven. Near the end, the left hand part is written in the treble clef.

A violin concerto is for a violin and an orchestra. This tune comes from the last movement (section) of Beethoven's concerto.

Air

This tune is by the English composer Purcell (1659-1695).

Listening to piano music

On the next page there is some music by the German composer Schumann (1810-1856). Schumann was also a piano player and a writer on music. You could listen to his Piano Concerto in A minor, and to his pieces for solo piano such as *Papillons* and *Carnaval*. He also wrote some less difficult music called *Album for the Young*. The pieces on pages 102, 108 and 120 of this book are from *Album for the Young*.

Humming song

When you see a note written as a quaver and a crotchet at the same time, hold the crotchet down for its full value, but keep the quaver line going as well.

This is another way of making you emphasize notes.

102

Make sure you play the notes of the left hand line in the correct clef. They are in the treble clef at the beginning, but the clef changes twice during the piece.

Musette

This tune is by Bach. It is from a group of dances called a suite.

This tune has a continuous note in the left hand called a drone. It imitates an old instrument called a musette, which was like bagpipes.

104

Greensleeves

This is an old English tune. It is also known as *The Blacksmith.* The time signature means there are six crotchets in a bar.

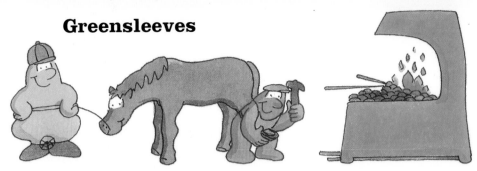

Pipe and drum

Changes of time and key signature

Sometimes the time signature changes in the middle of a piece. In this tune it changes from four to three quavers in a bar. It will be easier to change time signature if you count the quaver beats in your head. This is because the speed of the quavers remains the same throughout the piece.

The key signature of a piece can also change. When this happens, a new key signature cancels the old one. In this tune, play F sharps before, and B flats after the change.

Blue study

The lines above and below the notes in the last line are called *tenuto* marks.

You can find out more about tenuto marks below.

Tenuto marks

To play a note with a tenuto mark press the key slightly harder than usual, and hold the note for its full value.

A tenuto mark is a way of telling you to emphasize a note.

Melody

This tune is from Schumann's *Album for the Young.* Try to play it legato (see page 85).

Schumann was a concert pianist. However, he had to stop playing because he injured his hand.

Interpretation

Every performance of a piece of music is different. This is because there are many small changes you can make to alter the way the music sounds. You can play the music staccato, legato or a little faster, slower, louder or softer.

During your practice, try different ways of playing each phrase until you like the way it sounds. This is called interpretation. Interpretation gives your playing its own special character.

108

More about the sustaining pedal

Sometimes you can use the sustaining pedal even if it is not marked in the music.

You can use the pedal to play big jumps more smoothly.

Make sure that when you use the pedal, you only press it very gently.

Paris Quartet

This tune is by the German composer Telemann (1681-1767).

This sign is a trill. You can find out how to play trills below.

Trills

To play a trill, you play the note on which the trill is written and the note above it (see below).

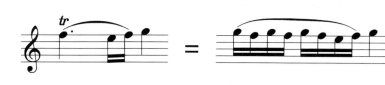

Alternate between the two notes for as long as the note with the trill on it lasts, like this.

110

Chorale

This tune is by Bach. It was written for the organ. You can find out more about the organ below.

Chorales can be sung too.

The organ

The organ is the oldest kind of keyboard instrument. Its sound is produced by pipes of different sizes, made from metal and wood.

Bach was a famous organ player. He wrote lots of music for the organ. Some of it can be played on the piano.

Minuet

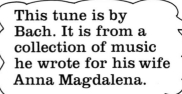

This tune is by Bach. It is from a collection of music he wrote for his wife Anna Magdalena.

The little notes in bar six are called grace notes. Find out how to play them below.

Grace notes

Grace notes decorate the music. Usually you play them just before the beat.

Don't play them too quickly.

112

Summer song

This tune has another kind of decoration called an *acciaccatura* ("a-chak-a-too-ra").

You can find out more about acciaccaturas below.

Acciaccaturas

The word acciaccatura comes from an Italian word meaning "to crush".

You play an acciaccatura as quickly as possible, before the note to which it is attached.

Scales and arpeggios

Scales are chains of notes that go up and down by step. There are two kinds of step in a scale: whole steps (tones) and half steps (semitones). A tone is made of two semitones put together. There are several kinds of scale. One of the most common is the major scale. The order of the tones and semitones in every major scale is the same. The steps between the third and fourth notes, and the seventh and eighth notes in a major scale are semitones. All the other steps are tones.

Arpeggios are spread chords. You can play them at the beginning of your practice, with the scale of the same key. The notes of an arpeggio are the first, third, fifth and the eighth notes of the scale in the same key.

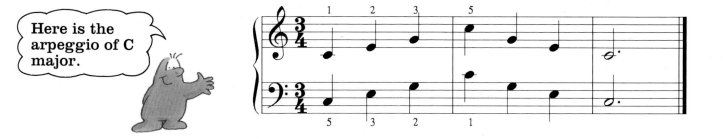

Here is the arpeggio of C major.

Scales and arpeggios of more than one octave

The scales on page 114 are one octave long. An octave is the distance between one note and the next note above or below it with the same name.

When you play scales and arpeggios, repeat them a few times by starting at the bottom of the piano and moving up through several octaves.

To play scales and arpeggios of more than one octave long, you need to change the fingering at the end of the first octave.

Below, you can play the scale and arpeggio of G major. Both of them are two octaves long.

Many of the pieces on the next pages contain parts that are based on scales and arpeggios.

Rondo

In a rondo, the first tune you hear comes back several times during the piece, with new tunes in between.

This tune is by Mozart.

The left hand plays in the treble clef at the beginning of this tune.

The groups of semiquavers will become easier if you play them slowly at first.

Waltz

This tune is by the Russian composer Tchaikovsky (1840-1893). There are E sharps in the third line. E sharp is the same as F natural.

The waltz is a German dance in $\frac{3}{4}$ time. It was popular in the 19th century.

118

Song of the reapers

Polonaise

This tune is by Bach. It is from the book of music he wrote for his wife Anna Magdalena.

The polonaise was first danced in Poland during parades and processions.

Andante

mf

mp

f

p

cresc.

In this tune you could try playing the quavers in the right hand part staccato, and the semiquavers legato.

My vineyard
(part B)

This tune is a duet (a piece for two people). It is based on a Russian folk tune.

Part B is played by the person at the lower end of the piano. Part A is played by the person at the top end of the piano.

My vineyard (part A)

It helps if you count a bar together before you start.

When you play duets, listen to the other person so that you play together exactly in time.

123

Humoresque
(part B)

This duet is by the Czech composer Dvořák (1841-1904).

Poco lento e grazioso means "quite slowly and gracefully". *Leggiero* means "lightly".

Poco lento e grazioso

p leggiero *cresc.* *dim.*

p *mp*

Ped. **Ped.**

Fine
rit.
Ped.

cresc. *dim.*

cresc. *dim.*

D.C. al Fine

Humoresque
(part A)

A humoresque is a lively, but also slightly sad tune.

Dvořák wrote eight humoresques for piano.

Index of tunes

Index